Higher Purchase

Rita Ann Higgins

By the Same Author

Goddess on the Mervue Bus
(Salmon Publishing, 1986)

Witch in the Bushes
(Salmon Publishing, 1988)

Goddess & Witch
(Salmon Publishing, 1990)

Face Licker Come Home
(Staged by Punchbag Theatre Co., 1991
& Published by Salmon Publishing, 1991)

God of the Hatch Man
(Staged by Punchbag Theatre Co., 1992)

Philomena's Revenge
(Salmon Publishing,   1992 - reprint 1993)

In memory of
Lily, Bim and Eileen

(Lily and Bim Donovan, Eileen Donoghue,
who died as a result of a tragic road
accident at Oranmore, Co. Galway in July 1995.
Lily was four months pregnant.
Eileen was eight months pregnant.
They were all members of the travelling community.)

Published in 1996 by
Salmon Publishing Ltd,
Knockeven, Cliffs of Moher
Co. Clare

A catalogue record for this book is available from the British Library.

ISBN 1897 648 987

Cover photograph by Mike O'Toole
Cover design by Fstresso
Set by Siobhán Hutson in Palatino
Printed by Colour Books, Baldoyle Industrial Estate, Dublin 13

Acknowledgements

The author is grateful to the editors of the following publications in which some of these poems, or versions of them, first appeared:

Stand (UK), Feminist Review (UK), Seneca Review (USA), Poetry Ireland Review, Southern Review (USA), Cyphers, Connacht Tribune, Galway Voice, Windows Publications, Deed (UK), Graph, Cúirt Journal, An Phoblacht (Republican News), UCG Students' Union Handbook, Finger Post (Derry) Clifden Anthology

Some of these poems have been broadcast by RTE radio and television. The title poem *Higher Purchase* was first broadcast on The Gerry Ryan Show, RTE 2FM. *The Temptation of Phillida* was first read on The Gerry Ryan Tonight Show (RTE TV). Excerpts from some of these poems have been read on RTE radio.

Special thanks to Phyllis and Dr. Noel Browne, The UCG English Department, Jessie Lendennie, Siobhán Hutson, Gráinne Healy, Anne Cavanagh and Tim Allen.

Contents

The Flogger   1

He Could Get Radio Prague   4

Impact '92   5

He Is Not Thinking About Last Night   6

Donna Laura   10

The Apple Tart Man   13

Higher Purchase   16

When the Big Boys Pulled Out   17

The Thistles   19

The Flute Girl's Dialogue   21

One for the Bus   23

The Trouble with Karen Reilly   25

Mothercare   27

The Quarrel   29

Burnt Offering   32

The Walkers   34

Whiplashed   36

Remapping the Borders   38

A Neck Ahead   40

Mamorexia   42

The Priest is Coming We Can Feel
   It in Our Bones   44

Easy Rider   47

The Winner   48

Breech   50

The Longford Slasher 51

The Taxi Man Knows 53

Diana Arrives at Monaghan Branch Library 54

When It Comes to the Crutch 57

Diotima Quirke 59

Always A Bridesmaid 61

Writer in Residence 63

Gretta's Hex 64

Prism 67

Tongue in Cheek 68

The Temptation of Phillida 71

The Nebulizer Gang 73

Delphi Lodge 74

Spiked 75

Changing Buses at Athlone 78

Night Noon and Nora 82

The Flogger

A man with such a belly
can never ever become a flogger
The Trial – Kafka

He wanted to be a flogger –
not just any old
swing the taws
Tom-Jack run-o-the-mill flogger
he wanted to be
the best flogger in town.

His father, a fines administrator
his mother, a fine administrator's wife
he knew about the letter of the law.

He longed to flog.
He would flog miserable souls
to within an inch of their miserable lives.

He fancied they would go away galled –
but confident that they were flogged,
not by any Jack-Tom chancer flogger.

They would respond to
how's she cutting greetings,
'flogged' they'd say,
'not by any run-o-the-chancer flogger
by the foulest flogger in town,
and furthermore it was a Double

1

Special Offer Monday flogging
me and the wife together
me with the left hand
the wife with the right hand
our agonies complete.'

When the town flogger
sullied his career
by blind dating a one-time flogged soul,
the fines administrator's son
took the reins.

The slim back
was his favourite
the back to tear a shirt from
the cat-o-nines-delight.

But this flogger,
not just any
swing the mill
run-Jack-over-Tom flogger
was a very fair flogger.

He always gave the choice
'take it off or have it torn off,'
that won him acclaim
that, and his Special Offer Mondays.

Like ever good flogger
he had his faults,
he had five stomachs

he had to keep them filled
he dipped often into other people's pots.

Eventually he got caught,
his father, a fines administrator
his mother, a fine administrator's wife.
The flogger, the fair old flogger
the 'take it off or have it torn off' flogger
got fifty lashes
inferior lashes by his standards,
the shame of the flogger
being flogged left its mark,
especially when he met
souls he had flogged
and flogged well,
his shame left him smaller
and red all over.

He Could Get Radio Prague

When he said
he could get
an oil rig for scrap
just like that,

and that
he could get
Radio Prague
on his transistor,

and that
he never backed horses
each way or in a placepot
only on the nose
always on the nose,

and that
he knew rakes of really famous actors
because of all the films
he was extra in,

and that
he was only hangin' round here
until Peter, their Peter,
came over from Canada with the jingle,

and that
it wouldn't bother him one bit
if he never saw
this fuck arse of a town ever again,

no one at the bus stop anythinged him.

4

Impact '92

In Derry
a funny thing
happened
on my way
to the reading.

A sky
of a man
in mossy tomb-stone
or olive green
nursing
his well groomed
baby Heckler

asked me,
while his thumb
was stroking
his aggressive pet,

my name
my address
and funnier yet
where I was from.

Keeping his thumb
his tomb-stone green
his dynamic pet
his sky high
in my sights

I gave the correct answer.

He is not thinking about last night

He is sitting
on a bollard
his head in his hands –
rats and ladders
from liqui-land
hoping for
a lift to town.

Cars are passing him goodo.
He is thinking into his hands
'How am I going to get a lift to town
for the cure, Jesus Mercy Mary help'.

He wasn't even out last night
he was in with M spirit Esquire
gut rotter
cell begrudger
brain emptier
usher to oblivion.

He head-in-the-handed it so long
there was talk of a plaque,
mind you it was only small talk.

The dissenters say he dogged it
and no plaque should he get,
they said he should be plaqueless.

They had a main speaker
who shouted from the back
of a rejuvenated Hillman Imp.
At times they joined in.

Usually the main speaker let rip
'Plaque what plaque, plaque my eye,
did they give me a plaque
when I got cancer of the ear lobe
and my ear fell off,

not on your ninny,
cop yourself ons they gave me
and plenty of them.

Haven't you got another ear they shouted
listen more carefully
with the one you've got
and you might be better off,
some things aren't worth hearing
some things are better left unsaid
that's the type of plaque I got.'

In time the plaque went up
and as plaques go this one didn't
weather beaten it stayed like himself
long after hours and hours.

Still the cars never stopped
but they slowed to a crawl.
Usually the eldest would do the honours

unless the eldest was insane
or under the throes of botulism,
then it would fall to the second eldest.

Males had superiority on Sundays,
Tuesdays and every third Saturday
all other days females read first,
except when the interlopers
tried to get a piece of the action.

Then the townies
even the dissenters
would take on plaque pride.

A deep breath was taken first;
these are the very boyos
who said earlier
'plaque what plaque, plaque my eye',

now they are telling the interlopers
'if any plaque needs readin' aloud
in this town
we have the vehicles
and the voice power
so feck off to Loughrea, Lockjaw
or Monaghan town for yourselves'.

So this day, a Sunday,
the plaque was read
the vehicle, a rejuvenated Hillman Imp
the occupant, a show-off

wearing one ear and beaming
with plaque pride
(the interlopers were balking in the bushes),

'This man is not thinking about last night
night of passion how good it wasn't,
he is hoping one of you family albums
with the lattice vests
the gaudy shades
the tattoos,
will stop your tripod philosophies
your umbrella loins
your barium meals
your poxy cars
and give him a lift to town
for the cure Jesus Mercy Mary help,

before his
soap-box eyes
challenge onto his palms
tour guide up his sleeves
slip-jig round his wind pipe
hammer down the town without him and jive.'

Donna Laura

Petrarch you louser,
I'm here plagued with the plague
and you're off chasing
scab free thighs.

Milli is the only one
who stood by me,
not that you could say stood,
she blesses herself
a thousand times a day
her head always ground-ward bound
prayers and half prayers
tripping her as she goes.

She scalds the arse off me
with the hot bricks
she keeps pushing between the sheets.

Between the shivers
the high fevers
and the hot bricks
I'm beside myself with anxiety.

Francesco, remember that good Friday
in the church of Santa Chiar?
You nearly knocked a column
gazing at me
plague free at the time
I had hardly a pimple.

Milli, off your knees,
and fetch me that ointment and gauze
wet my lips while you're at it.

It was Easter before
we met again
those three days
like three lifetimes,
little did I know
that the sonnets
were oozing out of you
and little Madonna Laura
was sparking them off.

Milli don't forget
to wrap a clean rag
around my chin when I go
give up that snivelling
and keep them Aves to yourself.

Whenever there was
a whiff of Pope in the background
you no longer saw me
only chalices, gold embroidered cloaks
large tracts of land
and Bulls, loads of Papal Bulls.

O Petrarch, you poser,
you were always swaggering
in and out of the Papal courts.

As for the sonnets
you were seen tearing them up
and throwing them petal-like
around the marketplace,
the Pope thought your piss was lemonade.

Petrarch, may you get what I have,
whoever rolled back that stone
should have rolled it over your head.

The Apple Tart Man

His prey: Teenagers
on summer jobs.
He throws them
side of the mouth orders
tart terminology
and hell-hound glances.

He thinks they don't sus the cryptic
unless it comes out in rap –
House of Pain or *Snoop Doggie Dog*.

He tells them,
'You're cutting the tart too big,
cut smaller portions.
I didn't get where I'm not
by giving out
portions that size
give smaller portions,
but don't charge less.

If you cut it this way
you'll get ten portions,
that way you'll get eight
get ten always get ten
never get eight.

When you get eight
you'll have to pay
for the other two portions

not seen on the plate
and another thing, you're late.'

His god is Apple Tart,
his mother is dead
she got eight not ten
how in hell could she win,
he served her up
with leeches and cream.

He scrooged portion
after portion out of her
until one day
she flaked away
the pastry of pity
damned forever
she got eight not ten.

At her funeral
he told her,
'I told you so
get ten never eight
but you wouldn't listen
always ten I said never eight'.

Meanwhile the fourteen year olds
were snoop doggie dogging it up
to an icing frenzy.

They waited in vain
in dry lakes

in dimly lit corners
in confectioners' nightmares.

One day they got lucky
they met up with him,
his legs in the air
his head in a bin.
They recognised
his balding soles
his mean heel.

All eager for their age
the voices had it,
a Shantalla voice:
the skin off his tight arse
a Mervue voice:
let's quarter him
an Upper Salthill voice:
his trout head on a plate
one sensible girl
from outside the walls
had the last Claddagh word:

enough of this greed
lets go by the slice
we'll have ten never eight,
always ten never eight.

Higher Purchase

We saw them take
her furniture out,

the new stuff
her kids boasted about
six months before.

The Chesterfield Suite
the pine table and chairs
the posh lamp
the phone table,
though they had no phone.

When it was going in
we watched with envy
she told her kids out loud
'You're as good as anyone else
on this street'.

When it was coming out
no one said anything,
only one young skut
who knew no better, shouted,

'Where will ye put the phone now,
when it comes'.

When the Big Boys Pulled Out

In S. P. S.
we parted the nuts
we parted the washers
between this and lunch time
we smoked.

A nut in this barrel
a washer in that barrel
never a washer in with a nut
never a nut with a washer be.

After lunch
was much the same,
divide and conquer
nut and washer
no thought for cancer
we all smoked on.

We had plenty of
nut and washer jokes
but they were all played out
and only used
when a new girl started.

We were cruel
sending her for a glass hammer,
a bucket of compressed air.
Soon enough she was flashing the ash,
and goading us on an all out strike,
when we got dermatitis.

17

This decisive thinker won us over
in a hurry, making her part
of our nut and washer brigade.

Our fag breaks
became our summer holidays
when the Big Boys pulled out.

Now everything
was in the one barrel
butts, nuts, bolts,
washers, dryers
eye shadows
wedding dresses
bell-bottoms
hopes, dreams, fantasies
platforms,
Beatlemania,

Costa del Sols
where-will-you-get-work-now jokes
that were no jokes
Benidorums
all alore-ums.

Our fag breaks
became our summer holidays
when the Big Boys pulled out.
No further need
of our discretion
a nut here
a washer there.

The Thistles

She was all over the place sadness
up and down coal buckets
in and out of old overcoats –
tears in her lap.

She placed the meat
on two dinner plates –
sit over here
by the window
we sat over there
by the window.

All this meat
how could we eat it
how could we not eat it.

Outside
the thistles were taller
than teenagers,
what could we say
what could we not say.

We decided on,
it's a great year for thistles
we said it in unison.

She nearly rose,
she neatly spoke,
'When I heard

you were coming
I killed the fatted calf
I filled your plates
with the tenderest meat
but still you looked.

I can't possibly
let you go now
you'd head off to town
down to the long walk
the tell thistle tale walk
you'd tell everyone
Teresa Tilley
has thistles
bigger than teenagers.

No,stay a while
stay forever
and stare out
at my thistles
my lovely thistles.'

The Flute Girl's Dialogue

Plato, come out now
with your sunburnt legs on ya
don't tell me to play to myself
or to the other women.

'Discourse in Praise of Love' indeed.

Bad mannered lot,
even if I cough when I come into the room
it does not stop your bleating.
That couch over there seats two comfortably
yet every time I enter
there's four of you on it
acting the maggot
then if Socrates walks in,
the way you all suck up to him.

Small wonder Plato
you have a leg to stand on
after all the red herrings
you put in people's mouths.
You hide behind Eryximachus
and suspend me like tired tattle.

'Tell the Flute Girl to go' indeed.

Let me tell you Big Sandals
the Flute Girl's had it.
When I get the sisters in here

we are going to sit on the lot of you,
come out then gushing platonic.

The Flute Girl knows
the fall of toga tune
the flick of tongue
salt-dip hemlock-sip
eye to the sky tune
hand on the thigh tune
moan and whimper talk
dual distemper talk.

When you played I listened,
when I play , prick up your ears.

One for the Bus

I went to see him today
it wasn't easy,
we didn't get on.

Before I could sit down
he talked non stop prostate,
'But it's not like regular
hyena through the veins cancer
more of a lazy bugger
kind of meanders
they can cut him off at the pass'.

Sit down I was told.
'I will, thanks'.
(Dutiful daughter,
hardly a daughter at all).

'If Bernie could nip in
on her way to work,
my feet are falling off
she might bring up some socks,
heart of gold that one.'

He offered me a mint.
'I will, thanks.'
He told me about your mano over there,

'Never shut it all night
how can a man rest.'

He rhymed out his lotto numbers,
thumbing each finger.
He told me about the nurses
' *They all fancy me you know'*.

I asked him about the horses.

*'Don't talk to me about horses
they're running backwards
one let me down badly
in a Yankee yesterday,
the gennet'*.

More lotto talk,
*'England have the lotto now,
what they can't steal from us
they copy '*.

More mano over there talk
more when I get out things will be different talk
back then to safer ground;
a hurricane called Gordon is devouring Florida
a place for Irish weather
a place for every horse since Arkle
a race for mints.

*'Go on, go on I tell you,
take one, one for the bus.'*

The Trouble With Karen Reilly

She is mirror mirror
she is too much eye liner
she is lipstick redder than blood
she is Jon Bon Jovi
she is the salt.

Her skirts
way too short
her jumpers
way too low
and cheek
she could fire it
faster than lead.

If anyone called
she was ready,
she was always ready
set and she went
for spills and thrills

down the Falls
in a stolen car
a back seat passenger
with non stop gossip
of the weekend disco
who shifted who
who got the ride

she laughed for nothing
she sang for a hoot
'Everything I do
I do it for you'.

She was wild
she was free
she was Bon Jovi,

with the bullet in her back
she was Clegged.

Mothercare

The girls came over
to see the new buggy,
the rainbow buggy,
the sunshine stripes.

O.K. it was expensive
but it was the best
and welfare pitched in.

It had everything –
she listed its finer points,
underbelly things we hadn't seen.

A little touch here
and it collapses
a little touch there
and it's up like a shot,
you barely touch this –
and you're in another street
another town.

A mind of its own
a body like a rocket
it's yours to control –
just like that.

She swears she'll keep it well
immaculate, she says, immaculate.

When she's nearly eighteen
it will still be new,
Tomma-Lee will be two and a half,

she can sell it then
and fetch a high price,

almost as much as she paid.

The Quarrel

Zeus, loveen,
help me, help my son
who runs rings around me,
but not for long.

That rotten cur Agamemnon
has stolen his prize
and you know the way
our family gets about prizes.

Remember that time
we won the two turkeys at bingo,
they all said it was a fix
and I threatened to bring up
every last crab from the deep
to piss on their cabbage.

And you, you know all,
must know how I have defended you
against that Shantalla crowd
who call you The Bonking Swan
behind your lovely back.

Bow your head,
loving know all,
let everyone see the sign.
Show them die-hards
my invitation
didn't say don't come.

When Zeus bowed
his holy head
the heavens shook,
swans all over Sligo
were taking oaths
and cover, much cover.

Hera wasn't one bit pleased
'I see slithery feet was here,
begging as usual,
what did she want this time –
to plait your sable brows?'

Zeus tried to interrupt.

'Didn't I see her
with my own ox-eye
wrapped around your knees.

Fine thing
in my own house.
I can't glide into the kitchen
and have a cup of tea
and a kit-kat
but old slithery feet
has my tiles ruined,
well I'm fed up with it, by jingo.'

Just then Hephaestus appeared,
sick as a gone off mackerel
that the dinner would be spoiled

with all the quarrelling.
(Zeus nipped out for a solpadeine)
'Mother,' he said
'never mind that Barry's tea
drink this and swallow your resentments
you can't win against Zeus.

One time for nothing
he caught me by the foot
and hurled me into
the middle of next year
I'm still dizzy and lame.'

Hera laughed at this.
Apollo, mad to get
on The Late Late Show,
took out his harp, by Jove,
and they all drank nectar
till the bulls came home
and the craic was mighty
and Hera forgetting her jingo
let Thetis slide easy into the sea.

Burnt Offering

Betty loved to smoke.
Her favourite
a Silk Cut red
after dinner
with her feet up,
she looked forward to it
from about half twelve.

When her brother Frankie
got lung cancer
she promised
the Blessed Virgin,
no more cigarettes
if She let her brother live.

Frankie's cancer
got plucked out
by an Indian doctor with aplomb.
He was the talk of Tuam.

Frankie got younger and younger,
he started going line dancing
to discos, he loved the Rave
but he never touched E.
He went out with women half his age,
he stayed in with women half his age.
His hair grew back a different colour
everyone said he was a new man.
Fred Astaire, only younger
prancer, river-dancer.

Betty missed her one after dinner the most.
After about five years
she said to herself
the Blessed Virgin
can't remember everything,
and she had a smoke
and another and another.

That autumn
Frankie grew old
in a mad rush.
The younger women
wanted a faster tapper.
His hair fell like snow,
changing colour
before it hit the ground.
He thinned out and out
his shape was no shape.

Betty never forgave herself.
She was the talk of Tuam.

The Walkers

The seasons
she knows inside out
and the birds
by their first names.

She was too much
for the family
her nose always stuck
in the sun and stars,
the haste of light.

They spoke of her
in the seventh person
three times removed.

When she leaves
the hostel every morning
she walks without purpose,
but with speed,
holding the collars
of her coat
in a kind of
I'm-in-a-hurry way.

This day
like every day
she is going somewhere
in a great rush
never thinking about where her foot falls –
only how fast.

Late afternoon,
her gait less frantic,
she meets another collar holder –
destination: In-a-hurry-town
any-family-free-town.
She knows he has a long way to go
and he is only on the way there.

He kind of nods
she kind of nods
he gives her space.

She hopes from inside her collars
that he will never run out of ground.

Whiplashed

My client, your honour,
is experiencing great difficulty
sitting from a standing position
and standing from a sitting position.

His pelvic spring
is not what it used to be,
in fact on the night in question
his pelvic spring sprung.

His left trapezius muscle is trapped
and is starting to make encores
half two degrees south of his right hippus,
this carry on is involuntary.

Any examination of the throacic spine
activates the voice box,
and my client keeps repeating
in a sirloin staccato,

*Your numskull killed a swan
with my new numberella.*

Since the whiplash
my client is left-handed.
This makes shoe removing very difficult,
especially if you're in Dublin
and your shoes are in Cork.

Another thing, your honour,
since the lash
my client is unable to –
how shall we put it – flatuate.
This unfortunate condition
is causing a false fullness
which my client erogenously believes
will only be relieved
by forty lumber punctures.

Have you any idea, your honour,
the cost of a lumber puncture nowadays?

I implore your honour,
in your decision for compensation,

to think long and hard
about pelvic springing
which is still negative
despite 140 calls to
Orgasmic Orla
on the 'Let's Talk Dirty' line.

My client reminds me, your honour,
that before this pelvic punishment,
he was cock of the walk.

Remapping the Borders

In Texas
after the conference
they put on a céilí,
nearly everyone danced,
a few of us Margarita'd.

In jig time
everyone knew everyone.
After the Siege of Ennis
a woman asked me,
'Could you see my stocking belt
as I did the swing?'

I was taken aback.

Me, thigh, knee, no,
I saw nothing.
I saw no knee
no luscious thigh
no slither belt,
with lace embroidered border
that was hardly a border at all.

I was looking for the worm in my glass.

I thought about her after,
when I was high above St. Louis.
I'm glad I didn't see
her silk white thighs

her red satin suspender belt
with black embroidered border
that was hardly a border at all.

I swear to you
I saw nothing,
not even the worm
lying on his back
waiting to penetrate my tongue.

A Neck Ahead

Tesco the hip
was lucky.
He could feel
the stinging
where his hip broke,
it told him
when the frost was coming
or when his nag
was a neck ahead –
no forecast on the photo finish.

When his luck was in
sharp jabs hit a certain muscle,
this gave him hope
fresh pep in his step
the monetary pep.

His luck was uncanny
one day his horse won
the next day he won a horse.

Once he won claw hammers,
a thousand to be exact,
in mint condition.
A great joke
with the elbows on the wall gang
'The hip won the hammers'.

He didn't like it,
but he said nothing,
his worry was frost
mean frost,
coming hot and heavy.

He told the elbows,
'The frost is coming
next week you'll feel it –
you'll laugh claw hammers then,
a thousand of them
in pristine condition
on the other side of your cheek'.

Mamorexia

You should be
down on your knees
thanking God
with the lovely
husband ya have.

Look at Beatrice Cohen
the teeth nearly rotten
in her head –
what chance has she?

And her sister
spitting out babies
every time she coughs
and none of them
havin' any fathers,
except that lad
with the dark skin.

She was told often enough
no good would come of her
swanking round the docks
in those sling backs.

Lookit you
with those two angels
with them lovely
white bobby socks on them
and their father's eyes.

Cop yourself on –
your shadow looks
better than ya,
pull yourself together
and for crying out loud
go and eat something

something decent.

The Priest is Coming We Can Feel It In Our Bones

In the T. B. ward
we queue for the bath,
our bodies
are knackered
we are all skin and bone,
but the priest will give us
the body of Christ.

(This isn't just hearsay
sister Mary Mammary swears)

I'm the youngest
except for the epileptic,
she throws a fit
at the drop of a hat,
rolls her eyes
and rattles her head.

For her tantrum,
she'll get more of everything,
a spot of tea
a spot of toast
brown bread with
obscene amounts of butter,
sputum mugs full of glucose
white bread with
obscene amounts of butter.

You name it
we desire it
she gets it
all for a fit a fortnight.

Our spot is on the lung
we get to say ninety nine
ninety nine times
but no goodies
unless we rattle and roll.
Failing a fit,
our phlegm talk
must be convincing
otherwise we're out on our ear
with our bones in a bag.

The excitement is building
for the body of Christ,
our cheeks are flushed
our eyes are wide.

A pep talk
from Sister Mary Mammary –
to put zip in our loins
glucose in our mug.

'Come on now
he's landed,
throw shapes
not shadows
and remember

no shuffling
no profuse sweating
no farting
no fainting
no fits
and absolutely
no spitting.'

The priest is coming
we can feel it in our bones.

Easy Rider

He was always a rake
coming round corners
like his arse was on fire,

only the white
of his eye
and his denim jacket.

His mother's heart
was scalded
long before this,

and girlfriends,
girlfriends he had
but they never had him –
elusive Harley.

'Want a ride girl'
and you jumped on
and lived,

or you stayed behind
and lived to regret –
O Harley.

One sinister bend
broke his all
his brains were scattered
his blood rained.

Everyone said,
he died with his eyes wide open.

The Winner

It was his dog
you could tell the way
it clung round his neck
like a collar.

The remote control was his
his name was etched
with a broken penknife
across the top – His.

He always got
the biggest chop
when he was eating,
the biggest chop
he said, down boy down.

He spent all day every
burping and channel surfing
with his own ensignified remote control.

He was in Minnesota once
to check the time.
He always said,
'When I was in Minnesota
the chops were much bigger.'
He said it every day
chops, Minnesota, bigger.

His wife wished
and wished
that he would
go to Minnesota
and stick to
the biggest chop
and check the time.

He wasn't into divorce
or dirty dish washing,
he stayed and stayed
with his dog collar
his remote control
his greasy chop.

Got to hand it to him
on that remote control
he was fast,
he couldn't be beaten
he channel surfed all day,

at night he always came first.

Breech

In the maternity
'True Detective'
is passed
around and around,
talk breaks out
about the guy
who boils heads.

Everyone pitches in
a body under the floorboards
the bones of six
behind the dodgy wall panel
a fibula here
a tibia there,
mutilation becomes
an irregular verb.

I know no floorboard stories
I feel the odd head out,
we laugh it off
a pregnant pause,

razor-calm we go back to breast feeding.

The Longford Slasher

If anyone went in
before twelve
he would give his whistle
heart and lungs
and tell them
'Out of the pool now'
even if it was
two minutes to twelve.

One day a woman stood
up to her waist in water
she told him his whistle worked
and how she'd met his
two minutes to midday
whistle-blowing-Culchie-type before.
She thought she had him.

But he had people
they never had him,
except that one time
when the teacher told him,
'I expected more from you
and you getting the free books'.

That time he felt
the teacher had him
in front of forty potential swimmers.

He told the up-to-her-waister,
'It's not the ticks or the tocks love,
I'm not a clock-watcher
I don't come from clock-watcher stock,

in fact our Longfather clock
stood in the middle of the front room
upside down facing the telly
with its glass broken for years
until one bonfire night
they said have you anything,
that's how much we cared about ticks
tocks has nothing to do with it.

It's the ticket sister, you didn't show me your ticket'.

The Taxi Man Knows

I see them going off there
and hardly a stitch on them
one young thing
I swear to God
you could see her cheeks
another lassie
you could see her tonsils

and they come home then
crying over spilt milk

if she was my daughter
I'd give her something to cry over.

Diana Arrives At
Monaghan Branch Library

Soft day thank god
and nothing much is happening.
Any minute now
a man in a fierce hurry
will whir in here
looking for the time.

A woman, her hurry
equally fierce,
will ask for the Dundalk bus.

The librarian,
whose speed is always merciless
will say to him , will say to her:

'It's high time
you were behind bars
and I don't mean chocolate bars,
or do I look like the town clock?

Sorry mam we have no
Dundalk buses left over
could I offer you
a book maybe,
a newspaper even,
we do a great range
in Northern Standards'.

Before she gets a chance
the phone rings,
the beam is big
the news must be good.

There are three of us,
one reading The Irish Times
the other two
a Northern Standard apiece.

We lift our heads
host to heaven fashion,
we see ourselves
as beam interpreters.

The librarian,
still beaming,
puts the phone down.
Still beaming
she lifts it up again.

'Celine, hello, you'll never guess,

(We pause while Celine never guesses)

It's on its way
if you get in early
I'll stamp it for you,
this time tomorrow
you'll be edging on the epilogue.'
A longish pause,

A longish pause,
serene Celine
is saying something
we can't make out.

Serene Celine is reassured,
we, the Northern Standards and me
are relieved,
the beamer is beaming
her biggest beam.

'Don't you worry girl,
it will be here,
I've ordered two copies.'

When it Comes to the Crutch

Most of Joy-Roy-Gang
end up on crutches,
some die all of a sudden
some die all of the time
others join the Joy-Roy-Groupies Club,
they have afternoon crutch races.
Better than snatching
where the buzz is only part-time.

Hard chaws anyway
(look at Elvis Kelly
got a hook caught in his flesh
nearly lost his primer).
If you're on crutches
you're doubly hard.
So it is written on the fag wall:
Two legs good
Two legs with sticks gooder.

At the crutch race
this guy is hot, shit hot
hops like a pro, a real pro
he nearly always wins,
he jibes the others,

'Sissies, step-in-the-hallas
couldn't catch a wan-winged butterfly
with asthma, ye pussies'.

They know he's getting
too big for his boots
they all think it –
leaning against the fag wall.

The head crutcher,
(a right heel)
is losing face
he tells the asthma joker,

'You break
one of my crutches
I'll break
two of your legs'.

The leaners laugh last.

Diotima Quirke

Some people
would pay good money
to see a badger,
but not Diotima.
It's not that she doesn't like nature,
only yesterday she saw a magpie
take a rat by the scruff
and throw him at the sky.
The rat died.

Not that she ever saw a walking-round
hip swaggering badger,
only when a Toyota Starlet
had left the scene
the badger then looked like the rat
after the sky hit him.
The rat was obese.

The point was lawns.
D. couldn't give a curse
about African Lilies
or the chrysalis' of butterflies
or flowers that opened
and closed at will.
Her buzz was lawns
seamless lawns
eat your dinner off lawns
snooker table lawns

make love on lawns
(but no secretions please).

The problem was
the badgers liked golf.

Always A Bridesmaid

It was pay back
the Credit Union time again.

I noticed the notice board,
and why wouldn't I
I was bet up against it.

It was full
of bridesmaid dresses for sale.
'Lilac Satin bridesmaid dress
in immaculate condition
only worn once,
but not really worn at all.'

'Peach embroidered bridesmaid dress
for sale, one owner, silk sash and yoke
good nick except for port wine stain on the hem.'

I'm squeezing up the queue
trying to figure
the bridesmaid dress,
I can't make head nor tail.

Soon we'll have sayings unsaid, like
'She was a bridesmaid once'
'She was a bridesmaid and a half'
'Always a bridesmaid ...'

Has the bridesmaid had her day
Will the bride go it alone
hold her own train

61

throw her flowers
to horny bachelors
envious brothers
worst best men?

I get to the counter
I know by the way
she is sliding the hot cross pen
lethally over her right ear
that she wanted to become
a bride of Christ
but it didn't work.

A week before the wedding
she saw Jungle Jones
out jogging in his torn jeans,
the way he squeezed the coke tin
changes her mind, Christ could wait.

I asked her about the bridesmaid dresses.
She was quick off the mark
without wink or blink
she let me have it:

'If it's bridesmaid dresses you're after,
fill out a loan application like everyone else
we give no special privileges here,
this isn't the labour exchange,
and another thing
I'm from Renmore
not Gethsemane or Calcutta. Next.'

Writer in Residence

Learn from the start –
the porters
own the building
and if you want mail or keys
look lost sheep ahead
and play for a sugary execution
beg them, you are Mervue too
coax them to keep their daggered flicks
out of your simple life
swear to them
your little job
is only part-time.

Tell them the bank staff like you
how in the canteen you are first named
assure them *usit* Travel
have sent you places
and you have returned
fax them that spitting three times
in the clockwise
while holding your collar
might have worked
to disembowel the enemy
in the middle ages –
only two things are certain here,

the secretariat will never reach friendly
and the lift will not always have no memory.

Gretta's Hex

For years
Gretta cleaned
the factory
down the road from us.

When she had to have
her dog put down
because he had the mange

she got the runs
for three days.
Babbs Laffey
told the whole street.

Before this
she never missed work
not when her four girls
had the measles,
nor when the Pope came
to Ballybrit.

Now she went to the boss
she asked him for time off
to mourn her dead dog
she had long before the four girls
who recovered well from measles.

The boss said,
'Sorry Ann

64

I mean Gretta
I can't spare you now
what with Sadie,
I mean Annie, on holiday
and the two Mary's out sick,

you're the only one here
who can operate that buffer.
Can't you mourn your dead dog here,
take an extra fifteen minute
at tea break, good girl'.

All these foul noises
from the boss's mouth
upset Gretta
who never missed
a cleaning factory
four girls with measles
young people of Ireland
Pope filled Ballybrit day
in her life.

From her grief stricken
dead dog hole in the heart
she wished him:

Sightreducingweekendsahead
buffer festering
the company of bats
the company of bees (over-tired and hungry ones)
nouns with genitive singular inflection

verbs with janitor holding injections
slow dipping in the wallet (by others)
Sadie and the two Marys
and above all
sleepus interruptus with demonos oftenus
plus an extra fifteen minutes in hell.
Amen.

Prism

After the man
up our street
stuck broken glass
on top of his back wall
to keep out
those youngsters
who never stopped
teasing his
Doberman Pinscher,

he put
the safety chain
on the door,
sat at the kitchen window,
let out a nervous laugh,
and watched
the Castle Park sun
divide the light
and scatter it
all over his property.

Tongue in Cheek

Our driver
left us standing
in the rain
while he adjusted his seat,
he rose it
up and up
he tested it,
it fitted his five arses
like a glove.

He signalled out to us
a halting traffic signal,
'Hold on,' he said,
'wan more minute.'

It was only a soft rain
dripping from our frozen noses
onto our outstretched tongues
(that weren't really frozen at all).

We watched him bounce
on his high chair,
he checked his mirror
any minute now
we'd be in the fast lane.

He got out of the bus
locked the door
with the hand

behind the back hand.
(By nature he was
a back-hander,
by name, five arses).

'Wan more minute,
a quick leak,' he said
'just a leak, a lousy leak.'

Out dashed the back-hander,
by name five arses,
when the 3.10
from Ballina hit him,
he leaked.

The inspector broke the news
about our driver.
'My driver,' he said,
'I mean your driver
is very much under the weather.'

We wanted to somethingise
we really did
but our tongues were out
(now frozen)
we didn't know ourselves.

Not even our noses knew us
our families didn't know us
our friends didn't know us
our secret back of the car lovers

who bonked us down by the sliding rock
every Saturday night didn't know us,
our parish priest hadn't a bulls who we were
our local politicians didn't know us,
our family pets freaked and leaked.

We looked strange there
too long in the rain
our sympathy mangled
our tongues gone hard.

The Temptation of Phillida

When she was younger
much younger
she liked to look deep
into men's eyes.
A friend told her
men can make you come
with their eyes.

One day at the traffic lights
she saw eyes
she wanted to fall into.

The owner of these baby blues
was leaning against the jewellery shop window
sucking a woodbine.
She kept looking deeper and deeper
she could see sapphires, rubies, white gold.
Eternity rings, paternity rings
gold rings gold things
every conceivable carat
heart in hand rings
heart in bag rings
heart in honey rings
O honey.

'Do you fuck?' said the woodbine.

'Only men with big crocodiles,' she said.

He threw the butt down and walked away.

She called after him,

'Is your crocodile
finger licking good
or index finger big?'

He started to run.

The Nebulizer Gang

He knew when his chest made a sound
like a creaking door
that the rain was back
on his lungs.

If he didn't watch it
he'd be back
in the long ward
with the nebulizer gang
gassing about the new road diggers
you'd need to eat the hospital bread.
He'd tell every last oxygen masker
about Sheik Muhammad's horses
how they were winning here
because they spent all winter
on foreign beaches over in Dubai
wearing nothing but sun-glasses.

Lectures about living longer
and packing them in
were wasted on this old docker
who knew full well
a man had as much chance
of getting killed from the slap of a bus
or mangled in a runaway combine with no tax
as he had from sucking fuck
from a few lousy Woodbine.

Delphi Lodge *

If anyone told them
all of them
that one day
one Doolough day

a prince would come
not their prince
and eat *their*
eat well *their*
and sleep

the sleep of the dead *their*
and fish
fat fish *their*
from a graveyard
their graveyard,

they couldn't have walked any faster.

* In 1849, famine victims walked from Doolough to Delphi Lodge in Co. Mayo. They failed to get help from the board of Guardians who were meeting there. On their return, hundreds died, many were swept into Doolough Lake. When Prince Charles visited Ireland in June '95 he stayed at Delphi Lodge.

Spiked

On the way to court
they did the caterpillar crawl,
all hitting the same stride
jumpers hanging
long beyond the fingers.

They quarter-filled the court
'Grievous Bodily Harm'
was up again
this time it wasn't too bad
only assault with menaces
and a wheel brace.

The caterpillar crew hooted
when he back-cheeked the judge,
the judge warned
and warned again.

When the court adjourned for lunch
they sat in the long hall
on the back of seats
walkmans, talkmans,
gum gobblers,

Maria who and Kelly what,
Jimmy and Sonia
always a Sonia
praising their idol to the skies,

the leather jacket cut of him
how he sorted that judge
how he turned round
and gave the fist
bare faced
fearing nothing and no one.

More smoke
rings were made
butts were flicked in the air
a thousand curses
court was back in session.
'Grievous' made more jestures
finger and fist
and fist again.

The pillar crew were roused
they whistled
through their fingers
in unison
no calming them now,

'cept when the judge
passed sentence
giving 'Grievous'
four of the best
to be served on Spike.

Lower lips
were dropping
eyes were welling

mascara was getting smeared.
A girl with a spiral perm
addressed the court,

'I'll write
every day Grevie,
promise you will too.'

'Sure babe, why wouldn't I?'

He made a fist
with the free hand
he boxed the air
they cheered
he made a fist again,

soon the free hand
was cuffed
no more fist in the air
he gave them the chin.

They knew what he meant.

Changing Buses at Athlone

Abnormal abhorrent abysmal abominable
abrasive atmosphere in Athlone waiting room.

Backsliding barbed bureaucratic bacchanalia
in abundance in Athlone waiting room.

Cadre of cunning catharsissing Catholics
collapse corteging in Athlone waiting room.

Dastardly decked out dick heads dabble in
dare devil duck diving in the dirty day room
in Athlone waiting room.

Extensive extreme emotional emptiness exceeds
the exclamation of excruciating ecstasy never felt
in Athlone waiting room.

Filthy feelings full of finicky flat-footed flagellation
and foul words foreplay and fornicate in Athlone
waiting room.

Grandiose gravitating guttersnipes with gold toothed
good tempered good for nothing gonorrhoea who
gobbledygook and gawk in Athlone waiting room.

Hair trigger harlots with hatch men hatred and hard
core husky hybrid hunky dory hurling husbands hiss
hiss in Athlone waiting room.

Innumerable infectious insufferable irascible intestate inspectors inspect the intra-mural inscriptions on toilet doors in the Athlone waiting room.

Jellylivered Jack-in-the-pulpits jack-daws make je ne sais quoi jiffy jejune jaundiced jail jokes about how jinx the jittery janitor is in Athlone waiting room.

Kinky klutz the kat killer with knavish knick knacks knots the knitting and the knickers round the knees of killer kelly in Athlone waiting room.

Laudable long-legged laggards linger and lambast the lacklustre lackadaisical lamentation of the lustless languor of the lifesavers lying lifeless in Athlone waiting room.

Merciless mollycoddled mocking men from management with mostly moist mouths meander meaninglessly in misery through the maze of motionless mimics in Athlone waiting room.

Nauseating naive ne'er do wells who negotiate nepotism with nefarious nerds from nowhere which is neither here nor there in nearby Athlone waiting room.

Old-fashioned ominous obnoxious oblique odours occupy the orbicular organic oracular oddity with Iarnród uniform ossified in the corner of Athlone waiting room.

Piss-eyed pompous periwinkle perverts protest with placards about the pettifogging phoney phantom who plagiarises poetry in Athlone waiting room.

Quarrelsome quadrangle quarry workers in a quandary question the quota queuing for the quagmire, they also quib, query and quiver at ticket prices in Athlone waiting room.

Regiments of randy regressed religious relations rehearse relentless redhand rolfing relaxation remedies in Athlone waiting room.

Stoic stout-hearted sitting room socialists suggest stoppage as a stumbling block to the stubbornness of the stuck up staff in Athlone waiting room.

Thankless theatrical tridentine trickies in tricolours throb tired tid bits of timetable information through the tannoy in Athlone waiting room.

Unsavoury unmitigated utterances of unlimited unbecoming unemployment are ubiquitous in Athlone waiting room.

Visualise the vainglorious person whose vivid visionary visceral veins volunteered the plans for Athlone waiting room.

Wondrous were never the witticisms that wobbled from the warbled warlock's wallet while he watched and waited in Athlone waiting room.

Xanadu coated with Xanthene dye couldn't xerox from the mind the x-rated memories of Xmas in Athlone waiting room.

Yellow, not yeomanly was the yes person who yelled at the youth yahooing at the Yorkist who asked for yo-him-bine yoghurt in Athlone waiting room.

Zonked at the zero hour making zzzzz's like zombies with zilch results were the once zestful protestors in Athlone waiting room.

Night Noon and Nora

He was dead
no two ways about it
only his bones
never hit the clay
they were home
hitting the roof
when visitors came
he didn't want company
he only wanted her
not to leave him
to his thoughts
and his tea stained eyes.

Master of mime,
he put on fantasy stockings
he sat on fantasy chairs
he called her
night noon and Nora,
the woman he nearly married
forty years ago
the woman whose husband Pious
got back cancer
from carrying her troubles.

He went for a spoon
and he brought back a fish.
Once at Eyre Square, he cried,
'I don't know who I am
promise you'll never leave me Nora
even when I'm asleep.'

Her word was gospel,
she got tired nodding
but she never slept,
except for the forty winks last September.
She remembered every wink
like thick soup, she said.

She went to grief councillors,
she told them
bones in the house
spirit in the sky
stockings that aren't there
chairs that are no chairs
fish that are spoons
he's calling me Nora
I'm Bridget on the brink of a breakdown
help me.

They told her to let go
and let ever loving God
do night watchman.

The last straw was when
he turned up at second Mass
wearing only a lost look,
his clothes were at home
on the back of a chair,
a real chair.

She screamed out
to her ever loving God,

'I'm Bridget on the brink of a breakdown,
deliver me.'

God wasn't in at the time
he was down in Middle street
making mince meat out of Pious's cancer,
everyone knew that.